Laurence Hutton

Literary landmarks of Florence

Laurence Hutton

Literary landmarks of Florence

ISBN/EAN: 9783337111168

Printed in Europe, USA, Canada, Australia, Japan

Cover: Foto ©Andreas Hilbeck / pixelio.de

More available books at **www.hansebooks.com**

LITERARY LANDMARKS

OF

FLORENCE

BY

LAURENCE HUTTON

AUTHOR OF "LITERARY LANDMARKS OF LONDON"
"LITERARY LANDMARKS OF EDINBURGH"
"LITERARY LANDMARKS OF JERUSALEM"
"LITERARY LANDMARKS OF VENICE"

ILLUSTRATED

NEW YORK
HARPER & BROTHERS PUBLISHERS

Copyright, 1897, by HARPER & BROTHERS.

All rights reserved.

TO

CHARLES DUDLEY WARNER

MY FRIEND

IN FLORENCE AND ELSEWHERE

WHO FIRST ENCOURAGED ME

TO STUDY

THE LOCAL LANDMARKS
OF
LITERATURE

ILLUSTRATIONS

VILLA LANDOR	*Frontispiece*	
DANTE	*Facing p.*	4
VILLA PALMIERI	"	10
DEATH-MASK OF DANTE	"	12
VILLA GHERARDO	"	16
SAVONAROLA	"	24
SAVONAROLA'S CELL	"	26
MARTYRDOM OF SAVONAROLA	"	30
GALILEO	"	32
GALILEO'S HOUSE IN ARCETRI	"	34
GALILEO'S STUDY	"	36
PALAZZO DELLA SIGNORIA	"	42
LOGGIA DEI LANZI	"	54
TOMB OF WALTER SAVAGE LANDOR	"	58
CASA GUIDI WINDOWS	"	62
MRS. BROWNING'S TOMB	"	64
CASA BELLA	"	66
GATEWAY OF THE ENGLISH CEMETERY	"	70

INTRODUCTION

AFTER the article upon which this volume is based had been put into type it was carried to Florence, where it was carefully revised and not a little elaborated, many new items being added to it at the suggestion of Mr. Charles Dudley Warner, Prof. Willard Fiske, and others, whose local and antiquarian knowledge was of great value to me. It contains much information which does not elsewhere exist, in any collected form, and much more, which is the result of personal research and observation, never before printed in any shape. In the cases of Dante and Boccaccio, especially, I hope that I have succeeded in clearing up a number of doubtful points, and also in establishing more than one new and important fact not elsewhere on record.

The book is intended to be a guide to that particular side of the History of Florence, and of the Florentines, by birth and by adoption, which appeals more than any other side to me; and it is written for the sake of those who care to know how and when Florence was seen and enjoyed by those heroes and heroines of the pen whom we know and love through their works, from Dante and Boccaccio to Hawthorne and the Brownings.

I would rather have stood by the side of Dickens, on the Fiesolean Hill, when he caught his first glimpse of Landor's Villa, than have been a leader of the Guelphs or the Ghibellines who distracted Florence many centuries ago. In this light is the volume prepared, and for those whose tastes and sympathies are in accord with my own.

LAURENCE HUTTON.

HOTEL PAOLI,
Lung' Arno della Zucca Vecchia.

LITERARY LANDMARKS OF FLORENCE

LITERARY LANDMARKS OF FLORENCE

FLORENCE is still illumined by the reflected lights of its four great fixèd stars: Dante, who rose here; Boccaccio, who blazed here; Savonarola, who suffered here his cruel eclipse; and Galileo, who here peacefully set. Other planets have shone, and still shine, in its firmament, but towards these four great stellar bodies do the guides and the guide-books chiefly direct their telescopes to-day. If they were not all of them literary lights in the strictest sense of the words, they were, unquestionably, instrumental in casting much and lasting light upon the literature of science, humanity, and the beautiful.

Mr. Howells, in the delightful chapter entitled "A Florentine Mosaic," which opens his *Tuscan Cities*, says so much about Dante, in his house and out of it, that he has left— as is a way of his—little which is new or pertinent for those who come after him to say. He goes to the house, not far from Dante's, in which, according to tradition, lived Dante's wife, and to the house "just across the way," where, according to this same tradition, lived Dante's first and youthful love; he carries us to the neighboring church of S. Martino, in which tradition says that Dante was married; and everywhere he discourses most entertainingly and most instructively concerning what Dante did and hoped and suffered.

Dante was born in 1265; and a modernized house in the Via S. Martino, called "La Casa Dante," still bears a tablet to that effect. At the end of the fifteenth century this mansion is said to have been converted into a wine-shop, much frequented, then and later, by men like Michael Angelo and Benvenuto Cellini, perhaps for Dante's sake, perhaps for the sake of its Chianti; but a few years ago it was restored out of all decency; and now there is nothing left of what Dante knew and loved there but the sky above it and the earth beneath. Mr. Howells believes "that the back of Dante's house was not smartened up into Nineteenth-Century Mediævalism" as was its front, but the weight of antiquarian evidence, in this respect, seems to be against him.

It is not an easy matter for the stranger in Florence to find his way to the Casa Dante, even though he be equipped with the clearest of guide-books. It is in the heart of the city, and not very far from the Cathedral; but it is out of the beaten track of tourists; and the policemen in cocked hats, and the cab-drivers in hats of all sorts, do not always know where it is. Taking the broad Via Calzajoli—that is, broad for Florence—from the Duomo, and turning to the left into the narrow Via Tavolini, a continuation of the Via S. Martino, now called the Via Dante Alighieri, a step or two beyond the little Piazza S. Martino, you will come upon it; a tall, thin, commonplace house—No. 2 Via S. Martino—with an inscription over the door stating that here the Divine Poet was born, and an inscription on the door stating that the door is open to strangers on Wednesdays and Saturdays, from ten in the morning until three o'clock in the afternoon. The door itself, according to Dr. J. Marcotti, is placed where was no door in Dante's time; and even during the few hours of the week in which the latch-string hangs out the doorway is not worth entering. A flight of new stone steps conducts one to two small rooms, in the first of which Dante could not possibly have been born, unless he were born some six centuries after the accepted date of his birth, and in the second of which are a few very doubtful relics of the poet, some more than doubtful portraits of him, and a cast of his dead face which claims to be, and is not, the original mask.

Dr. Marcotti, usually reliable, inclines to doubt that Dante was married in the little church of S. Martino at all, notwithstanding the solemn allegations of the present custodian, and despite the fact that an ancient fresco there is said, by this very custodian, to represent the very wedding in question.

DANTE

UNIV. OF
CALIFORNIA

As Dante was undoubtedly born somewhere, so was he unquestionably married somewhere, and to somebody; and if he was not married in this particular church, we have no authority for believing that he was married anywhere else.

"There are stories that Dante was unhappy with his wife," writes Mr. Charles Eliot Norton, in his *Life of Dante*—edition of 1892, page 149; "but they start with Boccaccio, who was a story-telling gossip. He insinuates more than he asserts concerning Dante's domestic infelicity, and concludes a vague declaration about the miseries of married life with the words—'Truly I do not affirm that these things happened to Dante, for I do not know'!"

This same story-telling gossip is responsible for many other stories concerning Dante which have since been accepted as true, and concerning which nobody knows to this day. At all events, Dante's wife does not seem to have been a very comforting or a very comfortable lady to have lived with. She was the mother of four of his children, who were all of them homely, according to the traditional testimony of their father himself; and one of them was certainly named Beatrice. After Dante's expulsion from Florence his wife is said to have saved certain of his manuscripts from destruction; and the story runs that she sent the first seven cantos of *The Inferno* after him into his exile. This was not a little to her credit; and it is almost a pity that she never saw her husband again.

Dante's Beatrice, whom Boccaccio believed to have been a member of the Portinari family—which may or may not be the case—and who at the mature age of eight excited the tender passion in the bosom of Dante, then a mature youth of nine, lived with her father, according to the guide-books, on the site of the Palazzo Salviati, on the corner of the Via del Corso and the Via del Proconsolo; and—still according to the guide-books—in the court-yard of the present building there remains, to this day, a stone seat, in a niche in the wall, upon which, tradition says, the blossoming poet was wont to sit and gaze in rapture upon the nursery windows of the object of his adoration. They saw each other —still according to tradition—in the courtyard of her father's house, wherever it may have stood, at a May-Day Festival; and at first sight they were mutually attracted. No sooner met but they looked; no sooner looked but they loved.

Dante has put on record the impression she made upon him then. He tells how she appeared, and what she wore; and he adds— the translation is by Mr. Norton—"Though her image, which staid constantly with me, gave assurance to Love to hold lordship over me, yet it was of such noble virtue that it never suffered Love to rule me without the faithful consul of the reason in those matters in which it were useful to hear such consul." This must have been pleasant reading for the woman whom Dante married; and if it were found among the manuscripts which she preserved from fire by her care and devotion, it would prove that Dante was himself not entirely blameless for the incompatibility of temper which is said to have existed between them.

Signorina Portinari was married, to somebody else, before she was twenty-four; and Dante's Beatrice died in 1290. She was probably not the woman Dante imagined her to be; and it would have been a great deal better for Dante, and for all concerned, if he had not set the fashion of falling in love with, and rhapsodizing over, an ideal creature, which has since been followed *ad nauseam* by other poets not quite so divine.

The whole question of the status and condition of the Casa Dante is involved in mystery and conjecture, which is not relieved by the widely varying statements of the local guides. His family certainly lived in its neighborhood; their domicile not only having an entrance upon the Piazza S. Martino, but also one upon the Via Margherita, which runs by the side of what is now called the "Dante House," from No. 1 Via Dante Alighieri to No. 3 Via del Corso. But exactly where the domicile stood, and how much of it is now left, no person living can say; and all the doctors differ. Professor Cesare Calvi, of Florence, an enthusiastic and learnèd student of Dante and of his times, has devoted much care and thought to this portion of his subject; and to him I am indebted for the following hitherto unpublished attempt to unravel the tangle of words and of facts.

"The present House of Dante," he says, "has been rebuilt upon the site of a portion of the old house, which extended around to the Piazzetta della S. Margherita. The Donati had several houses, in one of which lived Gemma Donati, whom Dante married. These houses looked out upon the back of the present Piazza della Rena, which, in those days, was called the Donati Court-yard. They had one house, also, on the Corso, opposite the Church of S. Maria dei Ricci. Beatrice Portinari lived in a palace on the Corso, afterwards called the Palazzo Cepparello, where now the Fathers Scolopi have their school." The site of this house of the Portinari is No. 4 Via del Corso, some fifty or sixty paces from the Via Proconsolo, and some twenty-five paces from the little Via S. Margherita. It possesses a court-yard; but if it contains a stone seat or a niche in the wall, where the juvenile lover of the thirteenth century could have sat and mooned, such a niche and such a seat are not visible to the naked eye, or through the spectacles, of the Literary Pilgrim of the nineteenth century.

Beyond the Porta S. Gallo is a meadow, or grove, which once belonged to Dante, and which was a favorite spot of his in summer evenings, where he walked and pondered, and made *anni* rhyme with *sganni* and *posse* with *grosse*, without any interference on the part of his wife. It now forms a portion of the garden of the Villa Bondi, formerly the Villa Camerata, standing on the Via della Piazzola, just beyond the small Dominican convent which is on the right as one goes towards Fiesole. It is very close to the Villa Palmieri, or Villa Crawford, so intimately associated, by tradition, with Boccaccio.

Dr. Marcotti says that it is a well-known fact that the Alighieri family owned much property on the hill of Camerata, and he adds that at the time of the celebration of the six-hundredth birthday of Dante it was

clearly established, by positive documents, that the Villa Alighieri was, during the early years of the fourteenth century, that which was later known as the Garofano. During the period of Dante's banishment this property was confiscated by the state, and afterwards returned to the Alighieris, who sold it, in 1332, to the Portinaris, the family to which Beatrice is asserted to have belonged; and they, in their turn, disposed of it in 1507. The arms of the Portinaris are still visible upon certain portions of the house, and the Portinaris seem to have restored and renovated it during the fifteenth century. Owing to the antiquarian interest of Signor Bondi, into whose possession it came later, its original style and conditions have been carefully preserved.

"Dante's Stone," upon which, according to tradition, the poet sat and gazed upon the cathedral, then in course of construction, is itself of traditional authenticity, because little more than the lowest foundations of the Duomo had been built in Dante's time. The stone is still preserved, however, and, for safekeeping, it has been placed in the wall of the house numbered 30 Piazza del Duomo, on the south side of the square. It is a few feet above the street level, and when the present chronicler last saw it, or tried to see it, it was entirely covered by election posters; showing the power of politics over poetry even in Florence at the end of the prosaic nineteenth century.

We are hardly inclined to think of Dante as a Path-Master or Street Commissioner; nevertheless, recently discovered documents show that in 1301, just after he had served his term as Prior, a petition was presented to the six officials who had charge of the public roads, squares, bridges, etc., of Florence requesting that a certain thoroughfare should be widened and extended, and that Dante was appointed to oversee the whole matter.

The most interesting relic of Dante in Florence, except of course the famous, alleged, cast of his dead face in the Uffizi Gallery, is the mural portrait in what was once the chapel of the Bargello. For many

DEATH-MASK OF DANTE

generations it was covered by repeated coatings of the whitewash which the Italians are so fond of using in the wrong places, and it only saw the light again through the zeal and enthusiasm of Mr. R. H. Wilde and other American and English antiquaries, forty or fifty years ago. It is believed to have been painted in 1302, when Dante was in his prime; and, although it has been sadly abused, it is very precious in the eyes of all lovers of the lover of Beatrice.

Mr. Hare points out a number of the Landmarks of Boccaccio here: the site of "the darksome, sad, and silent house" in which he was born [?]; the Church of S. Stefano, between the Via Porta S. Maria and the Uffizi Palace, where he once lectured upon Dante's *Divine Comedy;* the Via della Morta, behind the Misericordia, which is the scene of a *Romeo and Juliet* sort of tale by Boccaccio; the old tower of the Palazzo Manelli on the corner of the Ponte Vecchio (No. 1) and the Via de' Bardi, just at the end of the bridge, where he spent many happy hours with his friend Francesco de' Amanetti, who is said to have made a copy of the *Decameron* from the original manuscript. But, curiously enough, Mr. Hare does not allude to Boccaccio's association with the Villa Palmieri near S. Domenico, and on the old road to Fiesole, where a choice party of ladies and gentlemen are said to have spent some time, during the plague of 1348, in the telling of choice stories for each other's amusement. This fine old country-seat, now called the Villa Crawford, and a favorite Florentine residence of Queen Victoria, is on the Via Boccaccio, on the right-hand side, and about half-way up the hill, as one goes, by the Porta S. Gallo, towards Fiesole. It has many terraces; and it is guarded by ancient statues of Italian gentlemen and ladies of Boccaccio's day, who strike one, as they struck Mr. Howells, as being plastic representations of the very members of high life who so long ago narrated Boccaccio's tales of deep and lasting love. They are far away from the electric cars, which run to and from Florence and Fiesole—in Boston style. And the prosaic nineteenth century has not yet succeeded in robbing them of any of their fourteenth-century charm.

The Villa Gherardo, or Villa Ross, on the Via Settignanese, and about half-way up the hill towards the little village of Settignano, just at the outskirts of Florence, also lays claim to the *Decameron*. It is a fine old château, of large size and with beautiful gardens. It dates back to the tenth century; it has a terrace of its own, and it is approached by a long, winding avenue, thickly hedged by bushes of luxuriant roses. It is now occupied by Mr. Henry Ross, an English gentleman, who has made horticulture his particular and very successful study, and by Mrs. Janet Ross, his wife, equally distinguished in the study of letters, who is the daughter of Lady Duff-Gordon, and the youngest of three generations of very remarkable women.

In this villa, Mr. Mark Twain, their near neighbor in the winter of 1892–93, entertained, more than once, a select company of ladies and gentlemen with the stories of

Jim Woolf and *Huckleberry Finn*, while the influenza, in a mild form, was raging in the city at their feet. Mr. and Mrs. Ross prove very conclusively, from local tradition, and from Boccaccio's own description of the Villa Gherardo in the introduction to the *Decameron*, that theirs is the "stately palace, with a grand and beautiful court in the middle, upon a little eminence, remote from any great road, amidst trees and shrubs of an agreeable verdure, and two short miles from Florence," to which the story-tellers repaired on the now famous Wednesday, by break of day. The galleries and fine apartments are still "elegantly fitted up and adorned with the curious paintings" of which Boccaccio spoke; and around it are still "its fine meadows and most delightful gardens with fountains of the best and purest water"; while "the rooms are graced with the flowers of the season, to the great satisfaction of all who see them," even at the present time.

It will be remembered that at the end of the second day, which was Thursday, Neifile, the new Queen of the Feast, proposed an

VILLA GHERARDO

CALIFORNIA

adjournment to another time and to another place; and that on the Monday morning early, "conducted by the music of the nightingales and other tuneful birds," they went "full west" by a little path, little frequented, to another beautiful palace situated also on an eminence and on a large plain. Here were "broad, straight walks, filled with vines; and in the middle of the garden was a plot of ground like a meadow; and in the centre of the meadow was a fountain of white marble." And so came they to the Villa Palmieri; and Signor Filostrato began the First Novel of the Third Day. The story is still extant, thanks, perhaps, to Amanetti's copy of the original manuscript, and is written in very choice Italian, hardly fit to be translated into the vitiated English of the end of the nineteenth century.

 The association of these two houses with the *Decameron* is further established by Baldelli in his *Life of Boccaccio*. He writes that the poet owned a small villa in the parish of Maiano, and that he was fond of describing the surrounding country, particularly the smiling slopes and rich valleys of the Fiesolean hills, which overshadowed his modest dwelling. "Thus," continues the biographer—"thus from the poetical picture which he draws of the first halting-place of the gay company, we recognize the Villa Gherardo, while from the description of the sumptuous palace to which they afterwards went, in order not to be annoyed by tiresome visitors, [do we recognize] the beautiful Villa Palmieri."

The confusion and the misinformation contained in the guide-books to Florence, of all languages and in all times, are too profound and too ingenious to be altogether accidental. When we are told that the site of the house in which Boccaccio first saw the light is now marked by an old fountain on the corner of the Via Guicciardini and the Via Toscanella, we consider the matter very simple; but when we find that the Via Toscanella and the Via Guicciardini run in parallel lines, and consequently cannot have a corner; and when we discover no sign of a fountain, ancient or otherwise, in either street, we sit us down, in some ancient doorway, in utter despair. And we are forced to conjecture that the ancient fountain in the Borgo S. Jacopo, just around the corner from the Via Guicciardini, and some steps away from the Via Toscanella, may, perhaps, be upon the sacred spot from which the author of the *Decameron* set out upon his illustrious career, until, after further research, we learn, upon excellent authority, that Boccaccio was not born in Florence at all!

Boccaccio certainly lived, and died, and was buried—for a time—in the otherwise uninteresting little town of Certaldo, about thirty-five miles from Florence, and on the road to Siena. His house, very much restored, and marked with a tablet, is still in existence there; and his fellow-townsmen, although they scattered his bones and broke his monument a century or so ago, still assert, and with proper pride, that he was born in their midst, mainly upon the strength of the fact that he called himself " Boccaccio of Certaldo."

That Boccaccio, the son of a Parisian

mother, was born in Paris and brought by an Italian father to Florence at an early age is, however, the generally accepted theory of the place and conditions of his birth. And this is the conclusion reached by Dr. Marcus Landau, a German biographer of Boccaccio, and a careful and conscientious student of his subject. He bases his belief upon circumstantial evidence, as well as upon Boccaccio's *Ameto*, which is, unquestionably, a slightly veiled account of the story of the poet's mother as told in later years by the poet himself. Nevertheless, Roberto Gherardo (Lord of Poggio Gherardo) left an interesting, and very prolix, manuscript account, written in 1740, of the house near his own estate, and called Villeggiatura di Maiano. He said (the translation is furnished me by Mrs. Ross): "In a small villa near Corbignano, now owned by Signor Ottavio Ruggeri, and which in ancient times belonged to Boccaccio di Chellino, and where he lived after he left Certaldo, his birthplace, to come to Florence, was born our Maestro Giovanni, whose birthplace, till now, it has been impossible to discover. I am the more convinced that our Maestro was born in this villa, because it lies about a mile distant from the valley of Ameto, where he describes himself, under the name of Ameto, as often visiting the Fairies and the Dryads who inhabited these forests, he being the child of the adjacent hills."

This may have been convincing to the Lord of Poggio Gherardo, in the middle of the eighteenth century, but I do not give it as convincing to a lord of a high-stoop brick house in Thirty-fourth Street, New York, at the end of the nineteenth century; and where Boccaccio was born, so long as he was not born in Florence, leaving a Literary Landmark here, on that account, it is not the purpose of this volume to discuss. That the Gherardi bought Pelagio del Poggio—"the House on the Slope"—in the year of our Lord 1342 and held it in their family until it came into the possession of Mr. Ross, a few years ago, it may not be out of place to mention here, as showing that the Italians do not, as a rule, "move" on the first day of every May.

The Villa Ross, unfortunately, was somewhat shattered and injured by the earthquake which picked up and shook Florence and its neighboring hills—for five seconds—in May, 1895, as a dog picks up and shakes a rat. The grand old tower of the Gherardi, which had stood for so many centuries, was so badly damaged that it had to be entirely demolished, for safety's sake, by human hands.

Petrarch is, naturally, associated with many of the cities of Italy; but in Florence, as his biographer expresses it, he seems to have "stopped only occasionally, to hold converse with his friends." Concerning his life here the histories and the guide-books are absolutely silent. We know, however, that his mother was born in the Palazzo Canigiana, on the Via de' Bardi. And there is a tradition—which is not an unreasonable tradition—that he was more than once an inmate of the Palazzo Manelli, so pleasantly associated with Boccaccio. No letter of Petrarch dated from Florence, or referring to Florence, is known to exist now.

Mr. Howells has not only foreclosed all literary mortgages upon the Meadow of Dante in Florence, but he has ploughed and harrowed the Landmarks of Savonarola here, and has sown and reaped a rich harvest. The gleaner of the after-math can only say that Savonarola sprouted and blossomed and bore his fruit in the hard, rough field of Florentine tares which ultimately crushed his body and set his great spirit free.

He entered the Convent of S. Marco here as a young man, when he created no particular impression either by his words or by his deeds; but when, some years later, he was appointed prior of the convent, he at once made himself heard and felt. He exhorted and scolded clergy as well as laity; and he preached purity of political as well as of personal conduct. And the more he was ordered by his superiors to be silent the more he talked. He was hissed and hooted, and pelted with curses and with stones. He was stretched, in the Bargello, upon the rack which tortured his body as cruelly as persecution had tortured his soul. He saw his two faithful monks slaughtered before his eyes; he was hung by the neck on the scaffold; and his body was consumed by fire while life was still in it; and still he preached. And still he preaches to all the world. "My sons," he said, in the library of S. Marco— "my sons, in the presence of God, standing before the sacred host, and with my enemies already in the convent, I now confirm my doctrine. What I have said came to me from God, and He is my witness in heaven that what I say is true.... My last admonition to you is this: Let your arms be faith, patience, and prayer.... I know not whether my enemies will take my life; but of this I am certain, that dead, I shall be able to do more for you in heaven, than living I have ever had power to do on earth."

Pope Pius VII., many years after Savonarola's death, is reported to have said: "I shall learn in the next world the mystery of that man. War raged around Savonarola in his lifetime; it has never ceased since his death. Saint, schismatic or heretic, ignorant vandal or Christian martyr, prophet or char-

SAVONAROLA

latan, champion of the Roman Church or apostle of emancipated Italy — which was Savonarola?"

Whether he was saint or heretic, prophet or charlatan, Savonarola and his memory are still honored in Florence; and his relics are never profaned even by political posters. The crucifix before which he is said to have knelt in prayer is still cherished in the Church of S. Michele; his portrait is still religiously kept in the Convent of S. Marco, where one still sees, now and then, on the priests in its cloisters, the white Dominican gowns similar to that in which he preached; and in the cells in the convent occupied by him in later life are preserved carefully not only his portrait, attributed to Fra Bartolommeo—and the best of him ever taken—but some of his manuscripts, portions of his wardrobe, his rosary, and a bit of charred wood, plucked from the fire upon which his body was consumed.

It was hoped that this might prove a memorial of Florence unique in its way, because of no occurrence of the name of the Medici. But as Mr. Dick could not resist the mention of Charles I., so can I not help a passing allusion or two to the family which for years forced themselves into every event connected with the history of the city. Ferdinand II. of that tribe, as will be seen, attempted to patronize Galileo; and Lorenzo the Magnificent, on his death-bed, was, according to tradition, severely snubbed by Savonarola. Dying in his villa at Careggi, the Magnificent Medici sent for the Fighting Prior, to whom he confessed as many of his greater sins as he could remember in so short a time. Absolution was promised on three conditions. First, that he should have a full and lively faith in the mercy of God. This was easy enough. Second, that he should restore all things he had unjustly possessed himself of. This was harder, but it could be done. Third, that he should restore liberty to the people of Florence. This was too much to ask, even of a dying man, and even in view of so glorious a reward. And the magnificent monk left the miserable Medici to go, unforgiven of priest, before the Final Judge.

SAVONAROLA'S CELL

It is only proper to observe here that considerable doubt has been expressed in regard to this story, which is based mainly on the statements of Savonarola's friends. Poliziano, who was with Lorenzo, says, simply, that Savonarola confessed the Medici, but retired without volunteering the blessing.

The beautiful Villa di Careggi lies outside of the Barrier Ponte Rosso, on the left. It is reached by the Via Vittorio Emanuele and the Via Macerelli. The name is on the gate; and not very much but the name is left of what Savonarola and the Medici knew of it.

Pasquale Villari, in his *Macchiavelli and his Times*, speaks in the highest terms of the intellectual qualities of the Magnificent Lorenzo, who seems to have been one of the wisest as well as one of the meanest of mankind. According to Villari, he was educated by the first men of letters of the age in which he lived, and he proved himself the equal of many of them in wit and in learning. He spent immoderate sums of money for the advancement of literature, while he gave himself up to dissipations which ruined his health and shortened his days. Learnèd men were employed in the public offices, and "from Florence, under his rule," says the historian, "spread a light which illumined the world. Lorenzo, with his varied and well-cultivated talents, his keen penetration and unerring judgment in all departments of knowledge, was no ordinary patron and Mæcenas; he stood among the first *literati* of his kind, and he took an active part in the labor he promoted, not only in the interests of his government, but also from real and undoubted intellectual tastes. . . . In his [own] poetry, as in everything else, he displayed great knowledge of human nature, and a fine taste, without, however, having sufficient elevation of mind to reach the heights of art. Even at that time [when he was in his eighteenth year] we find fine taste and ease in his verses, which are written in a spontaneous and something too popular manner."

Lorenzo, here accepted as a literary man, has left many landmarks in his native town.

He was born in the Palazzo Riccardi—then the Palazzo Medici—still standing at the beginning of the Via Cavour; and he is supposed to have been buried under Michael Angelo's "Twilight" and "Dawn," in the Church of S. Lorenzo, where he is represented as "The Thinker" by the same artist, a statue of which Hawthorne says: "No such grandeur and majesty have elsewhere been put in human shape"; and in which he will live for centuries after he is entirely forgotten as a man of letters or as a patron of the arts.

But to return to Savonarola. He was imprisoned in the Alberghettino, or little hotel — and an uncomfortable little hotel it must have been for him—a small chamber in the tower of the Palazzo Vecchio; and he spent the last night of his mortal life in the great hall of the Consiglio, or, as it is sometimes called, the Sala dei Cinquecento, erected for the meetings of the council established by his advice. He is said to have slept peacefully on the stone floor of this room, with his head pillowed on the knees of a faithful attendant; and on the morning of his **execution** he received the last sacrament in the Chapel of S. Bernardo, a beautiful little sanctuary well worthy of a visit for its own beautiful sake.

The scene of Savonarola's death, according to tradition and to the local guide-books, is on the site of the great Fountain of Neptune, by the side of the Palazzo Vecchio, in the Piazza della Signoria which, for many years, was known as the Piazza del Gran Duca. But the execution would seem to have taken place nearer the centre of the square, if any reliance can be placed upon an old and obviously incorrect representation of the event which is preserved in the inner of Savonarola's two cells in the Convent of S. Marco. The picture, a print of which is here produced, is not dated, but it was painted before the erection of the Uffizi Palace, in the middle of the sixteenth century, and it shows a long platform stretching from the corner of the Palazzo Vecchio, and from where the fountain now stands, but many yards farther towards the north, and about the site of

MARTYRDOM OF SAVONAROLA

the great glaring electric light of which Mr. Ruskin so justly complains. It should be mentioned here that most of the modern maps and plans of Florence are constructed with an eye for the picturesque, and without any regard to the natural and accepted points of the compass, the north and the south being rarely, if ever, on the top or the bottom of the documents.

Savonarola's ashes were gathered together at nightfall after the execution, and were cast into the Arno. Like the ashes of Wiclif, which were thrown into the river Swift, they have gone "into narrow seas, and thence into the broad ocean, and thus become the emblem of his doctrine, which is now dispersed all the world over."

Notwithstanding the pride of the Florentines in the possession of the bones of Galileo, he did in reality very little for Florence, except to come here to die. The oscillations of a hanging-lamp in the cathedral at Pisa, in which city is a tablet marking the site of the house in which he was born, gave him the first idea of the pendulum; and he first turned his attention to the thermometer, the telescope, and the microscope at Padua. When he was punished by the Inquisition because he said that the world moved, he sought refuge in Florence; and from here he went, peacefully and willingly, in 1642, to join the stars which he had brought so much nearer to the moving earth.

The Casa Galileo (on the south side of the Arno), No. 13 Costa S. Giorgio, in which Galileo lived for some years, is a long house on a sharp incline; two stories in height up the hill, three stories in height below. It is defaced by ugly modern frescos, and by a libellous portrait of its illustrious occupant. A military barrack is just beneath it, and crowds of children beg coppers of the Landmarker who sits him down in front of it to record his impressions, while their seniors look over his shoulder at the little book in which, to their great surprise, he is making notes and not a picturesque sketch.

The tablet on this house of Galileo seems to have been placed there, not to record the great fact that it *was* Galileo's house, but

GALILEO

UNIV. OF
CALIFORNIA

rather to record the utterly unimportant fact that once a certain member of the Medici family condescended to call upon Galileo here. And on the tablet on Galileo's house at Arcetri, near the famous tower, there is no hint given to the world that a greater than any of the Medici, one John Milton, a young English poet, destined soon to lose the sight of his eyes, came, in 1638, to visit the great Italian astronomer, grown blind already by weight of years and of sorrow.

Although one of Landor's *Imaginary Conversations* was that between Galileo and Milton on this occasion, neither Galileo nor Milton recorded, unfortunately, what was then said or done. It was unquestionably talk too good to have gone up the chimney or out of the window; and it is very hard for us, even with Landor's aid, to imagine it.

Galileo's Tower at Arcetri is well worthy of a visit, because of the view to be obtained from its top, if for no other reason. It is situated upon a commanding eminence, six or seven hundred feet above the Valley of the Arno; and it is reached by the Porta Romana, along the broad Viale di Poggio Imperiale, lined with its tall cypress-trees. Here are still preserved, in the study he occupied for many years, Galileo's microscope, many of his astronomical instruments, his portrait from life in pen and ink (it is supposed by Guido Reni) one of his autograph letters, the mask of his dead face, and other interesting relics. And by the rough wooden steps by which he himself climbed towards the sky one can now ascend to the square roof, to see the stars by night; and to see, by day, a vista almost unparalleled for beauty in all this revolving world in which we live.

Galileo's Tower forms a wing of a long, narrow mansion, beautiful and comfortable and cheerful enough, no doubt, in the summer months, but cold and carpetless and dreary enough in the bleak winter weather of Sunny Italy. It contains old and picturesque furniture, and frescos, and a few rare pictures, notably a portrait of Michael Angelo, attributed to himself, and a pencil sketch, by Canova, of the mother of all the Buonapartes; a family which, not being con-

GALILEO'S HOUSE IN ARCETRI

tent with having taken possession of almost all the rest of the world, still claims to have been indigenous to this soil.

The Villa Galileo, in which Galileo lived in Arcetri, while using the tower as his workshop by night and by day, and in which he died, is now numbered 23 Via del Piano di Giullari. It stands behind and below the tower, only a short distance away, and it is on the first turn to the right as one ascends to the Porta Romana. The house on the street side is commonplace enough, except for a baddish modern bust of Galileo, and for a tablet bearing the dates of his birth and his death. The "back of the house," as one of the guide-books expresses it, "fronts on a beautiful garden, and commands a most lovely view." His life there was saddened by domestic as well as by public trials, and was only occasionally cheered by such expressions of sympathy as men like John Milton could bring to him. The house does not seem to have been altered since Galileo died—in the year in which Newton was born. But as it is not "a show-place," and as permission to enter it is granted only by the courtesy of the present proprietor, a private gentleman, the present chronicler can only speak of it as he saw it from the little street; and he can only thank Galileo for having lived in it, and for having lived at all.

Both the house and the Tower of Galileo, at Arcetri, are now easily reached from Florence by the prosaic horse-car, which, like the Buonapartes of three-quarters of a century ago, has taken possession of all lands; and which is called, in all languages—except in the language which originally gave it a name —"the tram."

Galileo's body now lies in a magnificent monument in the nave of the Church of S. Croce. According to the Misses Susan and Joanna Horner, as set down in their admirable *Walks in Florence*, when Galileo's bones were removed there, in 1757, from an adjoining chapel, a titled and enthusiastic idiot cut off and carried away the forefinger and thumb of the right hand of the Master, in order "to possess the instruments with which Galileo had written his great works." Another fin-

GALILEO'S STUDY

ger, removed by another vandal, is said to be preserved in the room dedicated to Galileo at the Museum of Natural History here. Happily the head of Galileo, which directed these "instruments," was undisturbed, and now rests with what was left of his terrestrial body.

Many years ago Leigh Hunt wrote:—
"Above all, I know not whether the most interesting sight in Florence is not a little mysterious bit of something looking like parchment, which is shown you under a glass case in the principal public library. It stands pointing towards heaven, and is one of the fingers of Galileo. The hand to which it belonged is supposed to have been put to torture by the Inquisition for ascribing motion to the earth; and the finger is now worshipped for having proved the motion. After this let no suffering reformer's pen misgive him. If his cause be good, justice will be done it some day."

Milton came to Florence in the autumn of 1638, and he seems to have made many friends here, and to have been hospitably entertained. "In the private academies of Italy, whither I was favored to resort," he wrote, "some trifles which I had in memory, composed at under twenty or thereabout, met with an acceptance above what I had looked for; and other things which I had shifted, in scarcity of books and conveniences, to patch up among them, were received with written encomium, which the Italian is not forward to bestow on men of this side the Alps." Again he said:—"There it was that I found and visited Galileo, grown old, a prisoner of the Inquisition, for thinking, in astronomy, otherwise than the Franciscan and the Dominican licensers thought."

Milton came back to Florence in the spring of 1639, when, according to his own account, he was received with no less eagerness than if the return had been to his native country and his friends at home. He remained here two months on the second visit, and Masson believes that he saw Galileo again, and probably more than once.

While Amerigo Vespucci has no especial claims to Landmarks that are Literary, except as the writer of voluminous and excellent letters, the literature of a great nation owes to him at least a name; and some of its makers and its readers, on that account, if on no other, will perhaps care to know, when they come to Florence, just where he was born and lived. The site of his house on the Borgo Ognissanti—No. 18—and near the Via dei Fossi, is now occupied by a hospital founded by him. Here he wrote the letter which Martin Waldseemüller quoted in his *Cosmographiæ Introductio* in 1507, with the remark:—" Now a fourth part of the world has been found by Amerigo Vespucci, and I do not see why we should be prevented from calling it Ameriga or America." And thus did the local habitation which Columbus is credited with discovering for us get its name. A stone in the floor of a chapel in the adjoining church of Ognissanti bears the legend, in Latin, that it was once the property of Vespucci; and the broad avenue on the banks of the river, from the Ponte alla Carraia to the Piazza degli Zuavi, is called Lung'

Arno Amerigo Vespucci to this day — with no one to object.

Niccolò Macchiavelli is chiefly interesting to the students of English literature as having contributed two important words to the language. As Macaulay said, out of the surname of Macchiavelli we have coined an epithet for a knave, and out of his Christian-name a synonym for the devil; and, as *Hudibras* Butler put it:

> "Nick Macchiavel had ne'er a trick,
> Tho' he gave his name to our Old Nick."

Whether the devil in this case has received more or less than his due, it is not my place, or my purpose, or in my power, here to say.

The house in which Macchiavelli lived, and died, at No. 16 Via Guicciardini, and a stone's-throw from the Ponte Vecchio, on the south side of the river, has no less than two tablets to mark these facts, the later and larger one having been placed there in 1869, on the four hundredth anniversary of the great man's birth. The mansion has been cruelly done over, during the last decade or two, and its beautiful door was carried to the Tower of Galileo, where it is still preserved. The house, as it now appears, is commonplace and homely, but it is still a good enough house to have lived and died in, and its occupant no doubt found it so, after an experience worse than death in a Florentine jail.

Macchiavelli, poet, philosopher, critic, historian, orator, diplomat, was locked up for many months, and among the lowest criminals, in the Stinche, an ancient prison which has since disappeared, and the site of which is now occupied by the Accademia Filarmonica and the Teatro Pagliano, in the Via del Fosso, near the Piazza S. Croce.

Macchiavelli was buried in the Church of S. Croce. His monument, erected by public subscription many years after his death, is a tardy recognition of what he certainly did for his town and his country.

Opposite the house of Macchiavelli, in the Via Guicciardini, stands the house occupied by the historian Francesco Guicciardini, who gave his name to the street in which he was born and in which he lived for many years. He is believed to have died at Arcetri, where much of his literary work was done, Florence being no more kind to him than she was, in the olden times, to the rest of her literary sons.

The Misses Horner tell a pretty story of a flying visit made by Tasso once to the architect Bernardo Buontalenti. The poet, living at Ferrara, had heard of the production on the Florentine stage of his pastoral of *Aminta*, and that the success which it had met here was due, in a great measure, to the scenery painted for the occasion by Buontalenti. Elaborate settings have saved many a doubtful play since those days, a fact which dramatists are slow to recognize; but Tasso, nobler than some of the men who have come after him, rode all the way to Florence to thank the artist, whom he embraced and kissed upon the forehead; and he then left as suddenly and as unexpectedly as he had arrived. When playwrights embrace scene-painters in our day we can

PALAZZO DELLA SIGNORIA, WITH THE
TOWER OF THE VACCA

hail the dramatic millennium as having come again!

Buontalenti's house still stands on the corner of the Via Maggio—No. 37—and the little Via Marsili, on the left-hand side as one passes along the latter street from the Ponte S. Trinità towards the Piazza S. Felicità. But if the frescos of Poccetti, of which the guide-books speak, were on the outer walls of the building, they have been stuccoed and kalsomined out of all existence by later owners.

Montaigne visited Florence in 1580, staying at the Angel Inn, where the charges were seven reals a day for man and horse—Florence being considered the dearest city in Italy. A real is a Spanish coin, worth at the present time about five American cents.

At a festival here, on St. John's Day, he had an opportunity of seeing all the women, old and young, and he was obliged to confess that the amount of beauty at Florence appeared to him to be very limited. He remarked upon a Florentine custom of cooling wine by putting snow in the glass, which liked him not; and he recorded his having bought eleven plays and some other pieces, and the fact that he saw here a copy of Boccaccio's will, with a discourse on the *Decameron*, the will being printed *verbatim* from the original, which was written on a ragged bit of parchment.

John Evelyn recorded in his *Diary* that he arrived in Florence on the 22d October, 1644, being recommended to the house of Signor Baritiere, in the Piazza Spirito Santo, where he was exceedingly well treated. His life here was that of the ordinary observant tourist of the present day.

Thomas Gray and Horace Walpole were together in Florence for some fifteen months in 1739-40, and were the guests of Horace Mann, although they do not say where. They went to Rome, and probably to Venice, together, but no particulars of these visits are to be found in Gray's *Letters*, edited by Mr. Edmund Gosse, or in the published correspondence of Walpole, except that Walpole wrote once:—" I am lodged with Mr. Mann, the best of creatures. I have a terrace all to myself, with an open gallery on the Arno; and on either hand two fair bridges. The air is so serene and so secure [this was in July, 1740] that one sleeps with all the windows and doors thrown open to the river, and only covered with a slight gauze to keep off the gnats."

From this description one must infer that the British Embassy in those days was on the Lung' Arno, perhaps between the Ponte Vecchio and the Ponte S. Trinità; and it may be that the Hotel of Great Britain still preserves its name and still marks its site.

Walpole had "already become fond of Florence to a degree; it's infinitely the most agreeable of all the places I have seen since London," he said. He seems to have led rather a wild life here, and during the Carnival, in March, 1740, he wrote:—"I have done nothing but step out of my domino into bed, and out of bed into a domino."

Horace Mann spent a number of years in Florence as the representative of the British Government, and all students of the city and of its history should read his *Letters* to

Walpole, edited and condensed by Dr. Doran. They give a very striking and a very vivid picture of Florentine Women and Men, and Manners, and Politics, and Social Customs, between 1740 and 1786. He was greatly disturbed by the visits of the Old and the Young Pretender, and of Theodore, King of Corsica. He was familiar with all the gossip and all the scandal of the place; and some of his epistles read as if they might have been written in our own day. In 1742 he gave a full account of an earthquake, which happened, however, at Leghorn, not at Florence; and on the 12th February, 1743, he wrote:—"We have strange and melancholy doings here. Everybody is ill of the Influenza. And many dye, particularly among the poor people!"

Smollett came to Florence in January, 1765, and "lodged at the Widow Vinini's, an English house delightfully situated on the bank of the Arno." His landlady, who was a native of England, he found very obliging; the rooms were comfortable, and the entertainment good and reasonable. He gave no account of his personal experiences here, and he hinted not at the exact, or the approximate, site of the Widow Vinini's hostelry. He saw a large number of fashionable persons in Florence, he spoke of its "tolerable" opera, and he dwelt at length upon the habits of the aristocrats of Florence in entering into partnership with the shopkeepers, even selling their own wine by retail. And he thought it "pretty extraordinary that it should not be deemed disparagement in a nobleman to sell half a pound of figs, or a palm of ribbon or tape, or to take money for a flask of sour wine, and yet be counted infamous to match his daughter to the family of a person who has distinguished himself in any of the learned professions."

Alfieri lived and died in the Palazzo Masetti, on the Lung' Arno Corsini, No. 2, facing the river, and a few steps west of the Ponte S. Trinità; the tablet informing the passer-by that here "The Prince of Tragedy wrote for the glory and the regeneration of Italy." The younger Dumas, who made a pious pilgrimage to this house a few years ago, described Alfieri's apartments as being upon the second floor; and Alfieri said in his *Memoirs* that he took possession of them in 1793. He told the story of his own life here —" the air, the view, the comfort, exciting his intellectual faculties to the utmost." The Countess of Albany was his constant companion in this mansion; and he died, in 1803, with his hand in hers. In his final delirium he repeated one hundred verses of Hesiod, which he had read but once, and that in his youth; and he went out of the world in the midst of his work and in complete harness. Alfieri's monument, by Canova, in the Church of S. Croce, was erected in 1810 by the Countess of Albany, who herself lies in the same church, under a beautiful tomb of white marble. She survived him twenty-one years.

The authorities of Florence have been very liberal in their tablets to their illustrious dead, and unusually generous in their engraved testimonials to the illustrious strangers who have lived and died in their midst. These tablets are in all quarters of the town, and upon buildings of all sorts and conditions. They are almost as thick as were the autumnal leaves which strewed the brooks in Vallombrosa when Milton saw it in 1638, and generally they execute their purposes with a fair show of truth. They are, however, often very confusing to the blind pilgrim, led by blind guide-books, and sometimes they force him to stagger from side to side of the little thoroughfares, with his head in the air and his feet in the mud, which is sometimes deep in Florence. He cannot afford to let one of them escape him, and while he is searching in vain for the house in which Byron lodged or Hawthorne studied, he will stumble, perhaps, unexpectedly and much to his satisfaction, upon the house in which Mrs. Browning or Mrs. Trollope died; and he will thank the authorities for giving him so much help as that, although he will, in the meantime, have wasted many precious minutes in trying to decipher the name of some Giovanni Somebody of whom he never heard, and for whom he does not care.

Byron spent but a day in Florence on his

first visit, in 1817. He went to the two galleries and to the Medici Chapel, which he described " as fine frippery in great slabs of various expensive stones, to commemorate fifty rotten and forgotten carcasses. It is unfinished and will remain so." In 1821 he was here again with Samuel Rogers, but only for a short time, and he has left no footprints in Florence at all.

Shelley was in Florence for a few months in the winter of 1819–20. Florentine art and literature seem to have impressed him less than the natural beauties of the surrounding country; and of its inhabitants, native and foreign, he saw but little, living here, as elsewhere, almost entirely within himself.

Leigh Hunt came to Florence in the summer of 1823. In his *Autobiography* he wrote: "The night of our arrival we put up at a hotel in a very public street, and were kept awake by songs and guitars. . . . From the hotel we went to a lodging in the Street of Beautiful Women—Via delle Belle Donne— a name which it is a sort of tune to pronounce. We there heard one night a concert in the street, and, looking out, saw music-stands, books, etc., in regular order, and amateurs performing as in a room. Opposite our lodgings was an inscription on a house, purporting that it was the hospital of the Monks of Vallombrosa. From the Via delle Belle Donne we went to live in the Piazza S. Croce, in the corner house on the left side of it, next to the church of that name.... We lodged in the house of a Greek, who came from the Island of Andros, and was called Dionysus; a name which has existed there, perhaps, ever since the god who bore it. Our host was a proper Bacchanalian, always drunk, and he spoke faster than I ever heard. He had a 'fair Andrian' for his mother, old and ugly, whose name was Bella."

The Street of the Beautiful Women, at present writing, sounds better than it looks or smells. It is close to the Via Tornabuoni, and in the very heart of the town—a short, dirty, crooked, narrow lane, too narrow to afford more than half a sidewalk through more than half its length, and it is given over almost entirely to stables and to dealers in charcoal. The Beautiful Women who frequent it to-day, and who are to its manor born, are mainly distinguished for some actual or affected contortion of body, or for some disfigurement of facial feature which is their chief claim upon the charity for which they clamor. The inscription upon the Hospital of the Monks of Vallombrosa is still to be seen, faded and dim, and high in the air, on the house numbered 1 Via delle Belle Donne; and, naturally, the Hunts must have lodged at No. 2 or No. 4, both of which face it, and are almost the only habitable mansions left in the street; families of respectable but unintellectual cart-horses having now their residences on each side of them.

The Piazza S. Croce house, numbered 14 to 17, is not a very inviting domicile. It is sombre, four stories in height, and around the corner from nothing. It now forms a portion of an Industrial School of Decorative Art, in a quiet spot very far from the crowd which is so rarely madding in Florence, even in the liveliest seasons of the year.

A little later Leigh Hunt went to Maiano, a village on the slope of the Fiesolean hills, where he found the manners of the hamlet very pleasant and cheerful; and he said that the greatest comfort he experienced in Italy (next to writing a book) was living in that neighborhood, and thinking of Boccaccio as he went about. He speaks of the tradition that Boccaccio's father had a house at Maiano, and that the poet was fond of the place. Out of his windows Hunt could see the Villa Gherardo, the *Decameron* Valley of Ladies, a villa belonging to the family of Macchiavelli, and Settignano, where Michael Angelo was born; and he has often told with what pleasure he looked back upon it all in later life. Here he had the society of Seymour Kirkup, Landor, and Charles Armitage Brown. And Hazlitt, who came once to see him here, described him as "moulting." "My last day in Italy," Hunt wrote, "was jovial. I had a proper Bacchanalian parting with Florence. A stranger and I cracked a bottle together in high style. He ran against me with a flask of wine in his hand, and divided it gloriously between us. My white waistcoat was drenched into rose-color. It was impossible to be angry with his good-humored face; so we complimented one another on our joviality, and we parted on the most jovial terms."

In 1828 Longfellow took up his abode in a house upon the Piazza S. Maria Novella, close to the Church of S. Maria Novella, where, as he remembered, Boccaccio placed the opening scene of the *Decameron*. In November, 1868, he wrote to Lowell:—" We are in the Hotel Arno; we are sumptuously lodged in a palace on the Lung' Arno, within a stone's-throw of the Ponte Vecchio. My bedroom, looking over the river, is thirty-three feet by thirty, and high in proportion. I feel as if I were sleeping in some public square—that of the Gran Duca, for instance, with David and the Perseus looking at me. I was there this morning before breakfast; so that I fairly woke up there, and rubbed my eyes and wondered if I were awake or dreaming."

In January, 1869, Longfellow wrote:— " Florence was charming. We were there

LOGGIA DEI LANZI

only three weeks, but we are going back again. We had a beautiful apartment close by the Ponte Vecchio, and right in the heart of the mediæval town. Close by, too, was the little church of S. Stefano, where Boccaccio read his comment on Dante; and the Uffizi and the Palazzo Vecchio, and Giotto's tower and S. Giovanni. It was delightful to be there."

Benvenuto's Perseus stands alone in the Loggia dei Lanzi to-day; the Young David having been carried, perhaps for safer keeping, to the Academy of Fine Arts. The Square of the Gran Duca is now known as the Piazza della Signoria.

The Villa Landor stands on the road to Fiesole, a mile or so beyond the Porta Gallo and on the Via delle Fontanelle. The property, bought by Landor in 1829, has lately come into the possession of Professor Willard Fiske, who has enlarged and almost rebuilt the house, although certain of Landor's favorite apartments, notably the dining-room, the drawing-room, and Landor's bedroom, have been carefully preserved. Here he held his famous *Conversations*, imaginary and real, and from his windows he enjoyed that fair Florentine prospect which age cannot wither and custom cannot stale. Mr. Fiske has had a series of fine photographs made of the house as it was in Landor's day, a set of which he has presented to the British Museum. It was out of one of the windows of this dining-room, by-the-way, that Landor once, in a fit of rash impetuosity, threw his cook; a deed he always regretted, because, as he expressed it, if he had selected the other window, he would not have demolished a bed of tulips of which he was very fond! Landor's guests here were all the distinguished men of letters who came to Florence in his day; and in the same hospitable house are entertained now all the men and women of science, letters, and the arts who come to Florence from all parts of the globe.

Locker-Lampson, in *My Confidences*, wrote of Landor in his later life:—" I made Landor's acquaintance at the Florentine Villa. He was well known in Florence for the eccentricity of his opinions and the turbulence of his behavior. He lived by himself, and solitude may have rendered him savage. His little villa was poor and bare, but there was enough for the exigencies of contentment and obscurity, and the situation was beautiful. . . . I found him reading a Waverley novel, and congratulated him on having so pleasant a companion in his retirement."

On the 2d of April, 1845, Dickens wrote to Forster:—" I went up to the convent [at Fiesole], which is on a height, and was leaning over a dwarf wall, basking in the noble view over a vast range of hill and valley, when a little peasant girl came up and began to point out the localities. 'Ecco la villa Landora!' was one of the first half-dozen sentences she spoke. My heart swelled, as Landor's would have done, when I looked down upon it, nestling among its olive-trees and vines. . . . I plucked a leaf of ivy from the convent-garden as I looked; and here it is for Landor, with my love."

Landor died, in 1864, in the Via della Nunziatina, now Via della Chiesa—No 93— a poverty-stricken, shabby little street, which was never genteel. It is on what is here called "the other side of the river," and it runs from nothing to nowhere. It is peopled by wheelwrights and venders of vegetables, as poor as is the street itself; it has no prospect of anything that is not commonplace, and it is far away from everything that Landor could have loved, or that could have made life to him worth living. No. 93 is one of the few respectable residences in the street. It overlooks, from the upper windows, and despite the high wall, the gardens of S. Maria Carmine, which are not particularly cheerful; and it has no tablet but the tin sign of the insurance company which protects it from fire.

Landor lies under a flat white marble stone in the English Cemetery here, on the left of, and not very far from, the entrance. The inscription simply bears his name and records the fact that it is "The Last Sad Tribute of his Wife and Children."

Fenimore Cooper passed here the winter of 1837-38. He examined twenty or thirty palaces before he found lodgings to suit him.

TOMB OF WALTER SAVAGE LANDOR

And although he described his apartments at length, and his life in them, he gave no hint as to where they were. "In the spring of 1838," he wrote, "we left our palazzo, within the walls, and went to a villa called St. Illario, just without them." But that is all.

Some of Cooper's impressions of Florence are worth recording. "New York, which is four times as large and ten times as rich, does not possess a tithe, nay, an hundredth part, of its attraction. To say nothing of taste or of the stores of ancient art, or of the notable palaces and churches, the circle of living creatures here affords greater sources of amusement and instruction than are to be found in all the five great American towns put together."

The five great American towns will, unquestionably, grant the stores of ancient art and taste to the Tuscan capital, but they will hardly admit the overwhelming charm of her circle of living creatures.

Charles Lever came to Florence in 1847, and he lived, for several years, in the Villa S. Leonardo, on the Via S. Leonardo, and near the old church of S. Leonardo, beyond the Porta S. Giorgio. Here he wrote, among other novels, *The Martins of Cro Martin*, *Roland Cashel*, and *The Dodd Family Abroad*.

Mrs. Jameson made many visits to Florence, and spent, at different times, many months here. But the only hint she gave as to her address is in a letter written in 1857 from No. 1902 Via Maggio. She went then, and earlier and later, to the residence of Mrs. Trollope, who, a devoted whist-player, was bitterly disappointed at finding that Mrs. Jameson did not know one card from another. She permitted herself to be lionized, which in her very heart she hated; but in other respects her days here were very happily and very usefully passed.

Just at the top of the Piazza de' Pitti, as one goes from the Arno, and on the Piazza S. Felicità—No. 9—where it is entered by Via Maggio, is the Casa Guidi, in which Mr. and Mrs. Browning lived for many years, and where, in 1861, Mrs. Browning died. It is a four-storied edifice, perfectly plain in its exterior.

The tablet on the Browning house bears the following inscription, roughly translated: "Here wrote and died Elizabeth Barrett Browning, in whose womanly heart were united profound learning and poetic genius; and who by her verse wove a golden wreath between Italy and England. Florence, in gratitude, placed this memorial here in 1861."

In 1848 Mrs. Browning wrote:—"In fact ... we have planted ourselves in the Guidi Palace, in the favorite suite of the last Count (his arms are on the floor of my bedroom). Though we have six beautiful rooms and a kitchen, three of them quite palace rooms, and opening on a terrace, and though such furniture as comes by slow degrees into them is antique and worthy of the place, we yet shall have saved money by the end of the year. ... A stone's-throw, too, it is from the Pitti, and really in my present mind I would hardly exchange with the Grand-Duke himself. By-the-bye, as to street, we have no spectators in windows, just the gray wall of a church called S. Felice, for good omen."

George S. Hillard, in his *Six Months in Italy*, spoke of the pleasure he had in meeting the Brownings in their own house in Florence in the winter of 1847-48, and he said that a happier home and a more perfect union than theirs it is not easy to imagine. Browning's conversation he found like the poetry of Chaucer, or like Browning's own poetry simplified and made transparent. He spoke of the marks of pain already stamped upon Mrs. Browning's person and manner, of her slight figure, of her countenance expressive of genuine sensibility, and of "her tremulous voice fluttering over her words like the flame of a dying candle over the wick."

Here on the 9th of March, 1849, their son was born, and here, a few days later, Browning heard of the death of his mother, to whom he was devotedly attached.

In Florence Mrs. Browning wrote *The Casa Guidi Windows* and *Aurora Leigh*. To Mr. Milsand, Browning wrote from this house in 1858:—" My wife will add a few lines about ourselves; she is suffering a little from the cold, which has come late, not

CASA GUIDI WINDOWS

very severely either, but enough to influence her more than I could wish. We live wholly alone here; I have not left the house one evening since our return. I am writing — a first step towards popularity for me — lyrics with more music and more painting than before, so as to get people to hear and see."

"Mrs. Browning," said Hawthorne, "met us at the door of the drawing-room, and greeted us most kindly — a pale, small person, scarcely embodied at all; at any rate, only substantial enough to put forth her slender fingers to be grasped, and to speak with a shrill yet sweet voice. She is a good and kind fairy, however, and sweetly disposed towards the human race, although only remotely akin to it. It is wonderful to see how small she is, how pale her cheeks, how bright and dark her eyes. There is not such another figure in the world; and her black ringlets cluster down her neck and make her face look the whiter by their sable profusion."

The story of Mrs. Browning's death in this house in 1861 has been given in the *Life of*

Robert Browning. It is one of sad yet tender and even cheerful courage and sweetness, and need not be repeated here.

Mrs. Browning rests on the left of the main path as one enters the gate of the English Cemetery here. The monument is elaborate, but the inscription is simple enough—" E. B. B."

When Lowell was living in the Casa Guidi, or under what circumstance, or who were his neighbors, is not recorded; but he wrote, in 1874, from the "Albergo del Norte, Firenze," of the deep chord touched by the sight of "those old lodgings in the Casa Guidi, of the balcony Mabel used to play upon, and the windows we used to look out of, so long ago."

The Hawthornes came to Florence in May, 1858. In his *Life* of his father Mr. Julian Hawthorne writes:—" The Casa Bella, a floor of which we occupied from the date of our arrival until the first of August, was a fresh and bright looking edifice, handsomely furnished and fitted, built round a court full of flowers, trees, and turf. A terrace, pro-

MRS. BROWNING'S TOMB

tected from the sun by a rustic roof built over it, extended along one side of the exterior, and low windows or glass doors opened upon it. The house was all light and grace, and well deserved its title; a room giving upon the garden was used by Hawthorne as his study; and there, when not wandering about the genial, broad-flagged streets, or in the galleries and churches and public gardens, he used to sit and sketch out his romance—the English romance, I think, not the Italian one. He did not write very much as yet, however; the weather would have made it difficult to stay in-doors in the daytime, even had the other attractions to go forth not been so alluring; and in the evenings [Hiram] Powers or some other friend was apt to come in, or he visited Powers's studio, or went to Casa Guidi, near by, where the Brownings were."

Elsewhere Mr. Julian Hawthorne writes:—
"Such friends as Powers and Mr. and Mrs. Browning afforded all that nature and art could not supply; and the freedom from all present labor and all anxiety for the mor-

row gave an inward pleasantness to every moment. I believe this to have been upon the whole the happiest period of Hawthorne's life."

"The Casa Bella," wrote Hawthorne himself, " is a palace of three pianos ; . . . to me has been assigned the pleasantest room for my study, and when I like I can overflow into the summer-house or an arbor, and sit there dreaming of a story." The Casa Bella is now numbered 124 Via de' Serragli. It is on the right-hand side of the street as one goes towards the Porta Romana, and a few doors below the Torrigiani Gardens. It is still a fresh and bright looking edifice. And the summer-house, preserved intact, is still the spot in which one would choose, above all others, to sit and muse, and dream of a story.

In August the heat of Florence drove the Hawthornes out of the city; and they took the Villa Montaüto, the villa on a hill called Bello Sguardo, about a mile beyond the Porta Romana. "Near at hand," says the son, "across the gray groves of olives, was the

CASA BELLA

tower to which Mrs. Browning had attached her poem of *Aurora Leigh*, and Galileo's Tower was also visible from our battlements. . . . The Villa Montaüto was, as readers of Hawthorne know, the protótype of that of Monte Beni; though the latter is placed in another region." It was in this mouldering stronghold that Hawthorne wrote the first sketch of the *Marble Faun*.

Hawthorne has put on record that he saw Bryant here, at the Hotel New York, in 1858.

As Venice is the resort of German brides, so is Florence the paradise of spinsters of all ages and all climes. At five of the clock, of almost every afternoon of the year, the rattle of teaspoons is heard in every *pension* in the town, from Paoli's to the Villa Trollope; and there is consumed daily, at that hour, enough thin bread-and-butter to shingle the roof of Vieusseux's Scientific and Literary Reading-Room, in the Via Tornabuoni.

Mary Ann Evans, better known to the world as "George Eliot," when she first came to Florence was a spinster—as she herself acknowledged in probating the will of Mr. Lewes many years later—and without question she was the greatest of all the spinsters who were ever cheered in Florence by the non-inebriating cup.

George Eliot and Lewes arrived in Florence in May, 1860. "We took up our quarters in the Pension Suisse," she wrote in her *Journal*, "and on the first evening we took the most agreeable drive to be had round Florence, the drive to Fiesole." This probably was the Hôtel de Londres et Pension Suisse, No. 13 Via Tornabuoni.

A few days later she wrote to John Blackwood:—"We are at the quietest hotel in Florence, having sought it out for the sake of getting clear of the stream of English and Americans."

"Dear Florence was lovelier than ever on this second view," wrote George Eliot, in her *Journal*, May 5th, 1861, "and ill-health was the only deduction from perfect enjoyment. We had comfortable quarters on the Albergo della Vittoria, on the Arno; and we had the best news from England about the success of *Silas Marner*. . . . We arrived in Florence on the 4th May, and left it on the 7th June—thirty-four days of precious time spent there. Will it be all in vain? Our morning hours were spent in looking at streets, buildings, and pictures, in hunting up old books at shops or stalls, or in reading at the Magliabecchiana Library." This is a portion of the National Library in the Uffizi.

There is a tradition in Florence that she wrote *Romola* in the Villa Trollope, in the Piazza Indipendenza, now a well-known *pension;* and her rooms are still pointed out to the inmates, and still bear her name. The windows, one flight up, look towards the south; and when there is any sun in Sunny Italy it shines in all its Italian glory upon them. These rooms have since been occupied by Mr. Thomas Hardy—as is most fitting—and it would be pleasant to think of *Romola* and *Tess* as sitting down there in harmony together; but while George Eliot certainly called upon the Trollopes in this house, neither does she nor Mr. Trollope hint anywhere as to her having been their guest there, even for a night. And *Romola* was written and finished, entirely in London, in 1861, 1862, and 1863!

Trollope wrote, in *What I Remember*:— "I had much talk with George Eliot during the time — very short, at Florence — when she was maturing her Italian novel *Romola*." And later he said:— "In 1869-70 George Eliot and Mr. Lewes visited Italy for the fourth time. I had since the date of their former visit quitted my house in Florence, and established myself in a villa and small *podere* at Ricorboli, a commune outside the Florentine Porta S. Nicolò. And there I had the great pleasure of receiving them under my roof. . . . Their visit, all too short a one—less than a week, I think."

Thomas Adolphus Trollope and his mother came to live in Florence in 1843. "After some little time and trouble," the son wrote, "we found an apartment in the Palazzo Berti, in the ominously named Via dei Malcontenti. Our house was the one next to the east end of the Church of S. Croce.

GATEWAY OF THE ENGLISH CEMETERY

A.1

Our rooms looked on to a large garden and were pleasant enough."

The church stands between this building and the house which was occupied by Leigh Hunt twenty years earlier.

After his marriage to his first wife, Theodosia Garrow, in 1848, Trollope moved into the mansion which still bears his name, and where his mother died in 1863, and his wife two years later.

The Villa Trollope stands on the corner of the great Piazza Indipendenza and the little Via Vincenzo Salvagnoli, once the Via del Podere. It is a plain, three-storied edifice, bearing a tablet stating that in this house on the 15th April, 1865, died Theodosia Garrow Trollope, who "with the soul of an Italian wrote, in English, of the struggle and triumph of Liberty."

After the death of the first Mrs. Trollope her husband sold this house and moved into the Villa Emelia, No. 41 Via del Ponte a Ema and beyond the Porta S. Nicolò.

At the elder Mrs. Trollope's weekly reunions appeared every one of any note in

Florence, and many of no note whatever; but all were most kindly and most hospitably received; the lion-hunters no doubt, as is their way, often driving the lions themselves out into the jungle of their own domestic privacy.

Two low, simple, white marble stones, facing each other, in the centre of the English Cemetery, and on a narrow winding path to the left of the main path, as one enters the grounds, mark the graves of Frances and Theodosia Trollope. Latin inscriptions record their virtues, their names, and their ages; and they lie but a few feet from Landor, and almost immediately behind Mrs. Browning. Arthur Hugh Clough, Theodore Parker, and James Lorimer Graham, Jr., are their neighbors; and within that little cemetery's walls are contained the most sacred and the most realistic of all the Literary Landmarks of Florence to-day.

INDEX OF PERSONS

ALBANY, COUNTESS OF, 48.
Alfieri, Vittorio, 47–48.
Amanetti, Francesco de', 13–14.
Amerigo Vespucci, 38–40.

BALDELLI, Signor, quoted, 17–18.
Bartolommeo, Fra, 25.
Beatrice Portinari, 6, 8, 9–10.
Benvenuto Cellini, 2, 55.
Boccaccio, 1, 10, 13–22, 44, 53, 54, 55.
Boccaccio, quoted, 5, 16–17.
Bondi, Signor, 11.
Brown, Charles Armitage, 53.
Browning, Elizabeth Barrett, 60–64, 65–66, 67, 72.
Browning, Robert, 60–64, 65–66.
Bryant, William Cullen, 67.
Buontalenti, Bernardo, 42–43.
Butler, Samuel, quoted, 40.

Byron, Lord, 49–50.

CALVI, CESARE, quoted, 8–9.
Canova, 34, 48.
Clemens, Samuel L., 15–16.
Clough, Arthur Hugh, 72.
Cooper, James Fenimore, 58–59.

DANTE, 1–13.
Dickens, Charles, 57.
Dumas, Alexandre, Jr., quoted, 47–48.

"ELIOT, GEORGE," 67–70.
Evans, Mary Anne, 67–70.
Evelyn, John, 44.

FISKE, WILLARD, 55–56.

GALILEO, 1, 26, 31–37, 38.
"George Eliot," 67–70.
Graham, James Lorimer, Jr., 72.
Gray, Thomas, 44.
Guicciardini, Francesco, 41–42.

Guido Reni, 34.
HARDY, THOMAS, 69.
Hare, Augustus J. C., quoted, 13–14.
Hawthorne, Julian, quoted, 64–65, 65–66, 66–67.
Hawthorne, Nathaniel, 64–67.
Hawthorne, Nathaniel, quoted, 29, 63.
Hazlitt, William, 53.
Hillard, George S., quoted, 62.
Horner, Joanna, quoted, 36, 42.
Horner, Susan, quoted, 36, 42.
Howells, William Dean, quoted, 1–2, 3, 14, 23.
Hunt, Leigh, 50–54, 71.
Hunt, Leigh, quoted, 37.

JAMESON, ANNA, 60.

KIRKUP, SEYMOUR, 53.

LANDAU, MARCUS, quoted, 20.
Landor, Walter Savage, 53, 55–58, 72.
Lever, Charles, 59–60.
Lewes, George Henry, 68–70.
Locker-Lampson, Frederick, quoted, 56–57.
Longfellow, Henry Wadsworth, 54–55.
Lowell, James Russell, 64.

MACAULAY, THOMAS BABINGTON, quoted, 40.
Macchiavelli, Niccolò, 40–41.
Mann, Horace, 44–46.
Marcotti, J., quoted, 4–5, 10–11.
"Mark Twain," 15–16.
Masson, David, quoted, 38.
Medici, de', Ferdinand II., 26, 33.
Medici, de', Lorenzo, 26–29.
Michael Angelo, 2, 29, 34.
Milton, John, 33, 35, 37–38, 49.
Montaigne, 43–44.

NORTON, CHARLES ELIOT, quoted, 5, 7.

PARKER, THEODORE, 72.
Petrarch, 22.
Pius VII., quoted, 24–25.
Poliziano, quoted, 27.
Powers, Hiram, 65.

ROGERS, SAMUEL, 50.
Ross, Henry, 15, 16, 21.
Ross, Janet, 15, 16, 20.
Ruskin, John, quoted, 31.

SAVONAROLA, 1, 23–27, 29–31.
Shelley, Percy Bysshe, 50.
Smollett, Tobias, 46–47.

TASSO, 42–43.

Trollope, Frances Milton, 60, 70–72.
Trollope, Theodosia Garrow, 71–72.
Trollope, Thomas Adolphus, 70–72.

Vespucci, Amerigo, 38–40.

Villari, Pasquale, quoted. 27–28.

Waldseemüller, Martin, quoted, 39.
Walpole, Horace, 44–45.
Wilde, Richard Henry, 13.

INDEX OF PLACES

ACCADEMIA DELLE BELLE ARTI, 55.
Accademia Filarmonica, 41.
Alberghettino, 29.
Alighieri, Villa, 11.
Amerigo Vespucci, Lung' Arno, 39–40.
Ameto, Valley of, 21.
Angel Inn, 43.
Arcetri, 33–36, 42.
Arno, Hotel, 54.

BARDI, VIA DE,' 13, 22.
Bargello, 12–13, 23.
Bella, Casa, 64–66.
Belle Arti, Accademia delle, 55.
Belle Donne, Via delle, 50–52.
Bello Sguardo, 66–67.
Bernardo, S., Chapel of, 30.
Berti, Palazzo, 70.
Boccaccio, Via, 14.
Bondi, Villa, 10–11.

CALZAJOLI, VIA, 3.
Camerata, Hill, 10–11.
Camerata, Villa, 10.

Canigiana, Palazzo, 22.
Careggi, Villa, 26, 27.
Carraia, Ponte alla, 39.
Casa—
  Bella, 64–66.
  Dante, 2–4, 8.
  Galileo, 32–33.
  Guidi, 60–64, 65.
Cathedral, 3, 11, 12.
Cavour, Via, 29.
Cemetery, English, 58, 64, 72.
Cepparello, Palazzo, 9.
Certaldo, 19, 20.
Chiesa, Via della, 57–58.
Churches—
  Bernardo, S., 30.
  Cathedral, 3, 11, 12.
  Croce, S., 36, 41, 48, 51, 70–71.
  Duomo, 3, 11, 12.
  Felicità, S., 61.
  Giovanni, S., 55.
  Leonardo, S., 60.
  Lorenzo, S., 29.
  Marco, S., 23–25, 30.
  Maria Carmine, S., 58.
  Maria Novella, S., 54.
  Martino, S., 2, 4–5.
  Medici Chapel, 50.

Michele, S., 25.
Misericordia, 13.
Ognissanti, 39.
Stefano, S., 13, 55.
Cinquecento, Sala dei, 29–30.
Consiglio, Hall, 29.
Corsini, Lung' Arno, 47.
Corso, Via del, 6–7, 8, 9.
Crawford, Villa, 10, 14, 17–18.
Croce, S., Church, 36, 41, 48, 51, 70–71.
Croce, S., Piazza, 41, 51, 52.

DANTE ALIGHIERI, VIA, 3, 8.
Dante's House, 2–4, 8.
Dante's Meadow, 10–11, 23.
Dante's Stone, 11, 12.
Duomo, 3, 11, 12.
Duomo, Piazza del, 12.

EMELIA, VILLA, 71.
English Cemetery, 58, 64, 72.

FELICITÀ, S., CHURCH, 61.
Felicità, S., Piazza, 43, 60.
Fiesole, 10, 14, 55, 57, 68.
Fontanella, Via della, 55.
Fossi, Via dei, 39.
Fosso, Via del, 41.
Fountain of Neptune, 30.

GALILEO, CASA, 32–33.
Galileo's Tower, 33–35, 36, 41, 67.

Galileo, Villa, 35–36.
Gallo, S., Porta, 10, 14, 55.
Garofano, 11.
Gherardo, Villa, 15–18, 20–22, 53.
Giorgio, S., Costa, 32–33.
Giorgio, S., Porta, 60.
Giotto's Tower, 55.
Giovanni, S., Church, 55.
Giullari, Via del Piano di, 35–36.
Gran Duca, Piazza del, 30–31, 54–55.
Great Britain, Hotel, 45.
Guicciardini, Via, 18–19, 40–41, 41–42.
Guidi, Casa, 60–64, 65.

HOSPITAL OF THE MONKS OF VALLOMBROSA, 51, 52.
Hotels—
 Angel, 43.
 Arno, 54.
 Great Britain, 45.
 Londres, 68.
 New York, 67.
 Norte, 64.
 Suisse, 68.
 Victoria, 68.

ILLARIO, S., VILLA, 59.
Indipendenza, Piazza, 69, 71.

JACOPO, S., BORGO, 19.

LANDOR, VILLA, 55–57.
Leonardo, S., Church, 60.

Leonardo, S., Via, 59-60.
Leonardo, S., Villa, 59-60.
Loggia dei Lanzi, 55.
Londres, Hôtel de, 68.
Lorenzo, S., Church, 29.
Lung' Arno, 45, 54.
Lung' Arno Amerigo Vespucci, 39-40.
Lung' Arno Corsini, 47.

MACERELLI, VIA, 27.
Maggio, Via, 43, 60 *bis*.
Magliabecchiana Library, 69.
Maiano, 17, 53.
Maiano, Villeggiatura di, 20-21.
Malcontenti, Via dei, 70.
Manelli, Palazzo, 13-14, 22.
Marco, S., Convent, 23-25, 30.
Margherita, S., Piazzetta della, 9.
Margherita, S., Via, 8, 9.
Maria Carmine, S., Convent, 58.
Maria Novella,S.,Church, 54.
Maria Novella, S., Piazza, 54.
Marsili, Via, 43.
Martino, S., Church, 2, 4-5.
Martino, S., Piazza, 3, 8.
Martino, S., Via, 2-3.
Masetti, Palazzo, 47-48.
Meadow of Dante, 10-11, 23.
Medici Chapel, 50.

Medici, Palazzo, 29.
Michele, S., Church, 25.
Misericordia, 13.
Montaüto, Villa, 66-67.
Morta, Via della, 13.
Museum of Natural History, 37.

NEPTUNE, FOUNTAIN OF, 30.
New York, Hotel, 67.
Nicolò, S., Porta, 70, 71.
Norte, Albergo del, 64.
Nunziatina, Via della, 57-58.

OGNISSANTI, BORGO, 39.
Ognissanti, Church, 39.

PADUA, 32.
Pagliano, Teatro, 41.
Palaces—
  Berti, 70.
  Canigiana, 22.
  Cepparello, 9.
  Manelli, 13-14, 22.
  Masetti, 47-48.
  Medici, 29.
  Pitti, 61.
  Riccardi, 29.
  Salviati, 6-7.
  Uffizi, 13, 30, 55, 69.
  Vecchio, 29, 30, 55.
Palmieri, Villa, 10, 14, 17-18.
Piazza—
  Croce, S., 41, 51, 52.
  Duomo, 12.
  Felicità, S., 43, 60.

Gran Duca, 30-31, 54-55.
Indipendenza, 69, 71.
Margherita, S., 9.
Maria Novella, S., 54.
Martino, S., 3, 8.
Pitti, 60.
Rena, 9.
Signoria, 30-31, 54-55.
Spirito Santo, 44.
Zuavi, 39.
Piazzola, Via della, 10.
Pisa, 31.
Pitti, Palazzo, 61.
Pitti, Piazza, 60.
Podere, Via del, 71.
Poggio Imperiale, Viale di, 34.
Ponte—
 Trinità, S., 43, 45, 47.
 Vecchio, 13, 40, 45, 54, 55.
Ponte a Ema, Via del, 71.
Ponte Rosso, Barrier, 27.
Porta—
 Gallo, S., 10, 14, 55.
 Giorgio, S., 60.
 Nicolò, S., 70, 71.
 Romana, 33-34, 35, 66 bis.
Porta S. Maria, Via, 13.
Proconsolo, Via del, 6-7, 9.
RENA, PIAZZA DELLA, 9.
Riccardi, Palazzo, 29.
Ricorboli, 70.
Romana, Porta, 33-34, 35, 66 bis.

Ross, Villa, 15-18, 20-22, 53.

SALA DEI CINQUECENTO, 29-30.
Salviati, Palazzo, 6-7.
Santo, Spirito, Piazza, 44.
Serragli, Via de', 66.
Settignanese, Via, 15.
Settignano, 15, 53.
Sguardo, Bello, 66-67.
Signoria, Piazza della, 30-31, 54-55.
Spirito Santo, Piazza, 44.
Stefano, S., Church, 13, 55.
Stinche, Prison, 41.
Suisse, Pension, 68.

TAVOLINI, VIA, 3.
Teatro Pagliano, 41.
Tornabuoni, Via, 51, 67, 68.
Torrigiani Gardens, 66.
Toscanella, Via, 18-19.
Tower of Galileo, 33-35, 36, 41, 67.
Trinità, S., Ponte, 43, 45, 47.
Trollope, Villa, 60, 69-70, 71-72.

Uffizi Gallery, 12-13.
Uffizi, Palazzo, 13, 30, 55, 69.

VECCHIO, PALAZZO, 29, 30, 55.
Vecchio, Ponte, 13, 40, 45, 54, 55.

Via—
  Bardi, 13, 22.
  Belle Donne, 50–52.
  Boccaccio, 14.
  Calzajoli, 3.
  Cavour, 29.
  Chiesa, 57–58.
  Corso, 6–7, 8, 9.
  Dante Alighieri, 3, 8.
  Fontanelle, 55.
  Fossi, 39,
  Fosso, 41.
  Giullari, Piano di, 35–36.
  Guicciardini, 18–19, 40–41, 41–42.
  Leonardo, S., 59–60.
  Macerelli, 27.
  Maggio, 43, 60 *bis*.
  Malcontenti, 70.
  Margherita, S., 8, 9.
  Marsili, 43.
  Martino, S., 23.
  Morta, 13.
  Nunziatina, 57–58.
  Piazzola, 10.
  Podere, 71.
  Ponte a Ema, 71.
  Porta S. Maria, 13.
  Proconsolo, 6–7, 9.
  Serragli, 66.
  Settignanese, 15.
  Tavolini, 3.
  Tornabuoni, 51, 67, 68.
  Toscanella, 18–19.
  Vincenzo Salvagnoli, 71.
  Vittorio Emanuele, 27.
Victoria Hotel, 68.
Vieusseux's Library, 67.
Villa—
  Alighieri, 11.
  Bondi, 10–11.
  Camerata, 10.
  Careggi, 26, 27.
  Crawford, 10, 14, 17–18.
  Emelia, 71.
  Galileo, 35–36.
  Gherardo, 15–18, 20–22, 53.
  Illario, S., 59.
  Landor, 55–57.
  Leonardo, S., 59–60.
  Montaüto, 66–67.
  Palmieri, 10, 14, 17–18.
  Ross, 15–18, 20–22, 53.
  Trollope, 60, 69–70, 71–72.
Vincenzo Salvagnoli, Via, 71.
Vittorio Emanuele, Via, 27.

ZUAVI, PIAZZA DEGLI, 39.

THE END

www.ingramcontent.com/pod-product-compliance
Lightning Source LLC
Chambersburg PA
CBHW022141160426
43197CB00009B/1381